THE BANKING M&A INTEGRATION HANDBOOK

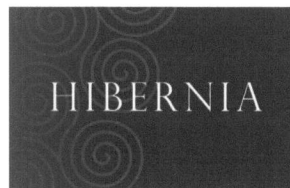

HIBERNIA

www.hibernia.pro

HIBERNIA CONSULTING LIMITED

Telford's Yard
6-8 The Highway
London E1W 2BS
United Kingdom

Tel: +44 (0)7879 404979
Fax: +44 (0)871 661 6645

Web: www.hibernia.pro

ISBN: 978-0-9559859-0-4

First Published in Great Britain 2008

© Michael McGrath 2008

Dedication

Orlaith, Andrew, James and Katherine

Acknowledgement

I would like to thank all those who supported and helped me in producing this book, including all my family and friends. In particular, Mary McGrath-Leahy for her excellent editing and Ebby John and Stan Oboisevs at CCCL for their assistance with producing the website and the marketing.

About the author

Dr. Michael McGrath is an established city professional, with over 12 years of experience of working for some of the world's leading banks, and prior to that 5 years working with IBM Research and Development in Stockholm. All of this time has been spent implementing complex change, in particular M&A management ranging from announcing the deal through to post merger integration. The main M&A deals he has worked on are:

- Lloyds TSB Registrars de-merger from Lloyds TSB Group
- Deutsche Bank acquisition of Dresdner Bank - Merger not completed
- Deutsche Bank acquisition of Bankers Trust - Then the largest banking acquisition ever
- Bankers Trust acquisition NatWest Markets - Then the largest banking acquisition in the UK
- IBM acquisition of Lotus Development

Additionally, he is probably the only person in the United Kingdom to hold a Doctorate in Banking M&A risk management. This rare mix of business acumen, practice and an advanced education allows him to combine the latest in management thinking and techniques with the practicalities of business reality. He has benefited from working at all organisational levels.

He has worked as a senior advisor and interim CIO since 2003. Prior to that, he was regional CTO for Corporate Technology at Merrill Lynch, and before that Head of Programme Management and Delivery at Deutsche Bank. His career in financial services began with JP Morgan where he was a global project manager and his technology career began with IBM where he worked in IBM's Nordic Lab.

.

Contents

Table of figures and illustrations

Introduction

Why you want to read this book

Have the champagne corks popped on a merger, demerger or acquisition affecting your company recently? Merging, de-merging, acquiring or acquired, if your organisation is involved or likely to be involved you will need to manage the process.

This is a simple straightforward handbook of how to manage the M&A integration process written by someone who has been responsible for managing the planning and logistics for some of the major deals of recent years. It shows you what has to be done before, during and after the change of control of a business unit of a whole bank from one owner to another.

Who this book is for

This book is for anyone who will have to plan, manage or execute the integration process. Whether you sit at the corporate headquarters or the individual business unit in the smallest region you will need to ensure your organisation, its processes and systems are understood and part of the overall integration effort for change of control (the cut over) and beyond.

While no two M&A deals are ever the same this will show you what you need to do and the questions you need to ask to make the integration successful on day one and thus set the stage for a successful post merger programme to realise the benefits of the deal.

It assumes you have a rudimentary understanding of project management. If not, I can recommend the sister book of this publication "The Project Management Handbook" available at http://www.projectmanagementhandbook.com/.

Benefits it will bring

You will be provided with clear approaches to all aspects of the M&A process. You will understand how failure intensive M&A can be, how a deal is executed and the steps involved. You will know the key stages involved and how they need to be executed.

Following the handbook will give you a clear simple framework to get the job done and help your organisation move on and attain the benefits and promise of the deal.

If that does not persuade you, consider this; this book is about controls and actions, which reduce failure to deliver the benefits of the merger or acquisition. Most mergers and acquisitions fail to deliver. Without these controls, you are stacking the odds on the side of failure. <u>You don't want to do that!</u>

Background

Failure intensive

M&A activity is a failure intensive activity. Some deals, even once agreed, are never completed. When such a falling apart of a deal happens it is often with significant consequences. In 1998 the merger of two pharmaceutical firms cancelled their planned merger. The share price of one dropped 8% and the other 15% that very morning. Sometimes after completion of the deal it becomes apparent the merger is not going to work. One US media merger resulted in the merged company writing down approximately US$60Bl of assets.

Most failures are not so spectacular. Merged companies fail to attain their original objectives. Estimates vary as to how widespread this is. Practitioner estimates suggest the failure rate is in the 70% to 80%[1] range. Yes, 70-80% of M&A activity will not result in the objective being reached. Quite a sobering thought! Therefore, in moving from agreeing a deal to completing the change of control and then moving from there to securing the M&A benefits, every reasonable effort needs to be taken to avoid failure. Evidence and experience shows that following the right processes and controls leads to reduced failure rates.

Activity

Overall M&A activity is on the rise, as this book goes to print, some are quite spectacular deals. Acquisitions such as Bank of America acquiring Merrill Lynch and Lloyds TSB Group acquiring Halifax Bank of Scotland and the demerger of parts of Lehman Brothers to Barclays Bank and Nomura are all signs that in good times and bad there can be demand of M&A activity among banks. These deals will contribute to another busy year for M&A activity.

---

[1] Spitzer, Kelly, Burns, Heckler, Prouty, Blum, Lloyd and Nardin (1999), *The New Art of the Deal* , KPMG, New York.

US M&A deal values (1968-2007)

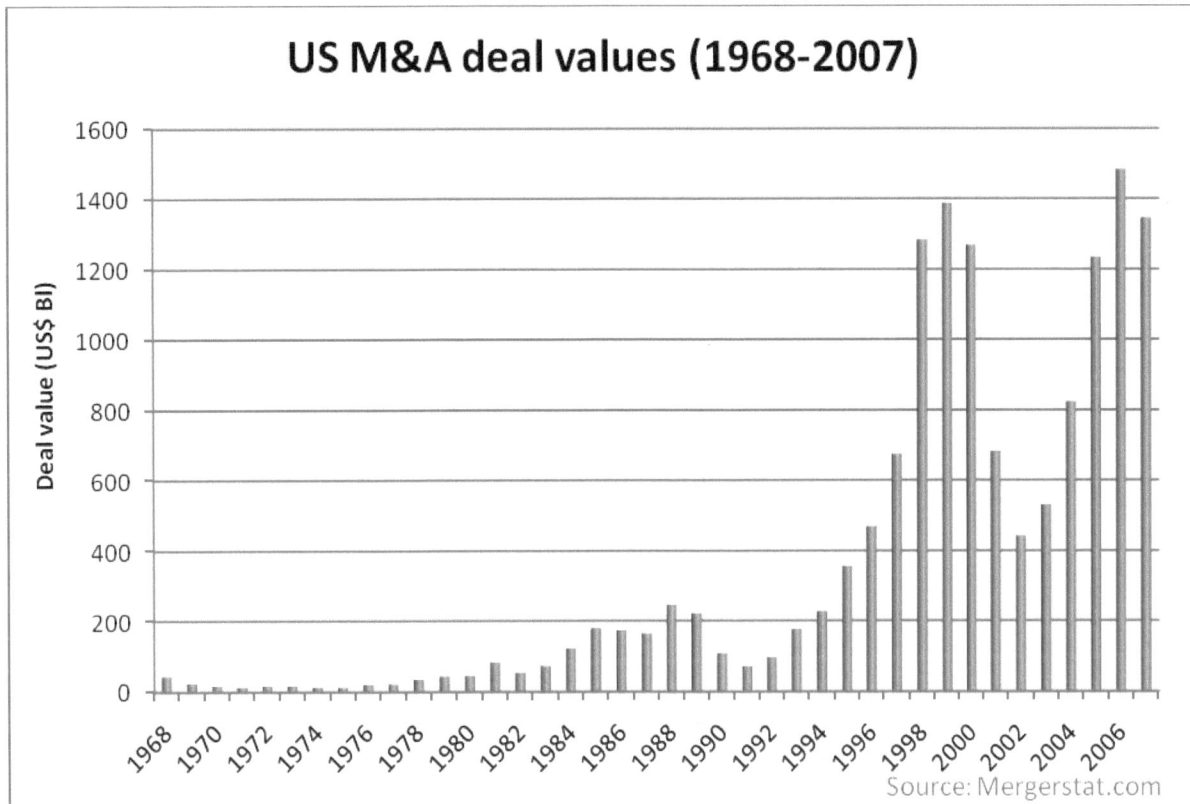

Figure 1 - US Merger deal (by value) 1968 – 2007

This growth in activity is not restricted to banking either. As you can see from the table above, M&A activity in the US for example, has been very strong over the last 20 years.

Reasons for M&A

There are many reasons firms engage in M&A activity. Reasons include:

- Maximises shareholder value – The value of the combined firm is greater than that of the two individual firms, even after the costs of the transaction and possibly a premium to acquire the target firm.
- Protection of the firm by virtue of size - The firm feels that by not increasing its size it may become vulnerable to market conditions or be taken over.
- To support growth.
- Acquire new markets, technologies or resources.
- May allow the firm to better manage capital or cash-flows.
- Management may also see personal benefits such as;
    - o A larger firm could improve their standing and remuneration
    - o They can deploy skills that are underused
    - o It diversifies risk leading to job security
    - o As stated earlier, it reduces the risk of being taken over and thus can also contribute to job security.

Anatomy of an M&A deal

Interaction of planning and actions

There are a number of strands of parallel activities that will happen during the integration period. These are summarised in the following figure:

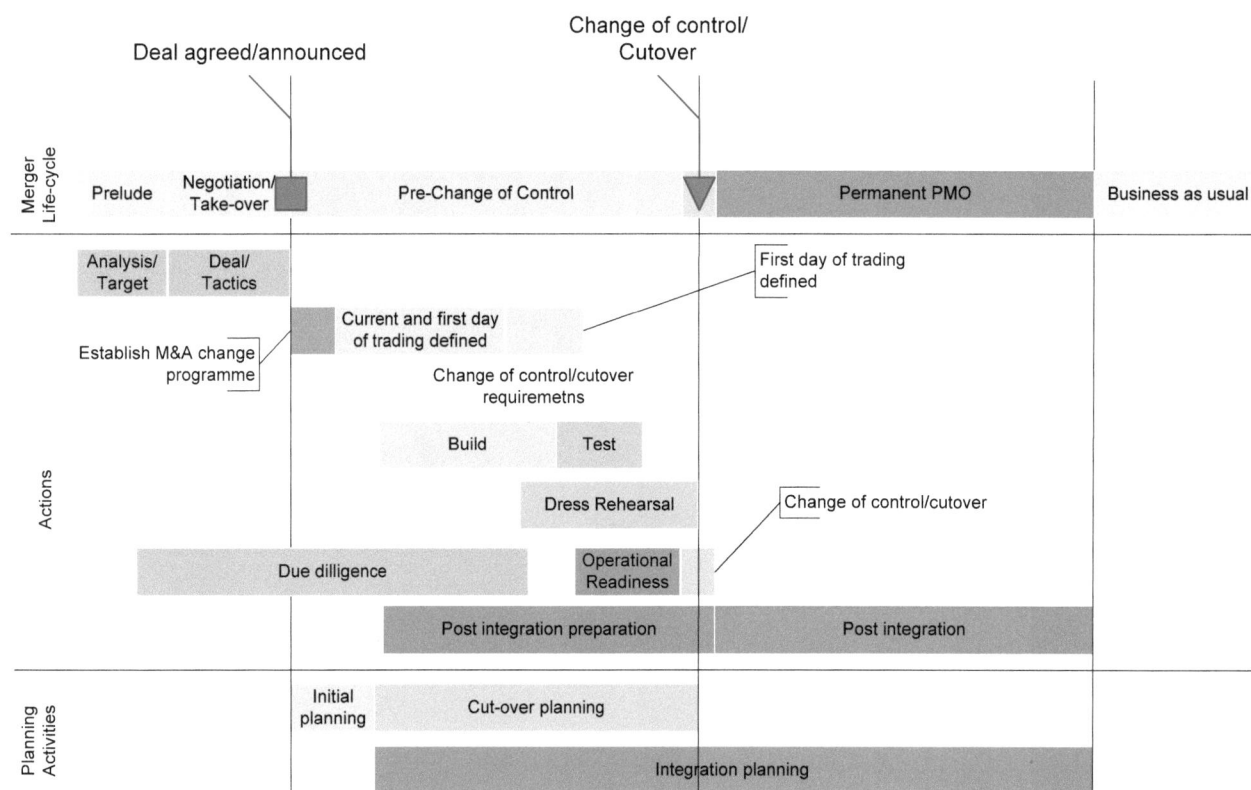

Figure 2 - Relationship of high-level planning

These activities are working to three major goals:

1. Bringing the two organisations together in such a way as to allow them to become a single legal entity
2. Legally and operationally effect change of control; and
3. Achieve the long term strategic benefits of the deal.

This book concerns itself primarily with the activities from the agreement of the team through to the successful execution of the cutover weekend, which includes the change of control itself.

The strands are usually undertaken by teams focusing on either due-diligence to make sure everyone knows everything in terms of values and there are no hidden problems. Those concerned with making the integration happen and those concerned with the post merger integration.

The planning and the corresponding actions will start with initiating the planning for the integration process itself, this will then evolve into detailed preparation for the change of control and executing the change of control event itself. Finally, there is the preparation for and subsequent execution of the post merger integration period.

Stages

An M&A deal progresses through a number of stages. These are:

- Prelude – This is concerned with the identification of the merger or acquisition target. Defining the type of organisation to target, identifying firms that meet these criteria and selecting the organisation you want to acquire or merge with. Sometimes this is a very analytical process, other times it is simply opportunistic; circumstances will dictate as will the companies' own strategic preference.
- Deal negotiation – Approaching the other company and agreeing a deal, or in the case of a hostile takeover, taking majority control of the company.
- Pre-change of control – This period is concerned with many activities. Completing due diligence to make sure the company is worth what it is thought to be worth. Keeping the two organisations functioning effectively. Preparing for the change of control (seeking regulatory approval, for example). Preparing the ground for post-merger activity. Decisions made on post merger approach and strategies will impact how the change of control weekend (cutover weekend) is progressed.
- Change of control – Legal transfer of ownership, plus making sure the organisation can operate as a single entity
- Post merger integration – The longer term programme of change to realise the benefits of the merger or acquisition; and
- Business as usual – The organisation is no longer executing the merger or acquisition.

The first two steps can involve many diverse activities such as negotiation and bidding tactics, valuation and identification of how future value can be achieved. We are concerned with the process of integration, typically our story starts with the announcement of a deal to buy or merge or even to de-merge (take part of the business out and sell it as a stand alone entity).

Timing

Timing is crucial. If you do not feel a continuous sense of urgency you are probably doing something wrong. Time is of the essence, once the deal has been announced, you need to prepare for the change of control and the post merger integration period when the value of the merger or acquisition will be realised. The post merger period starts the second the legal act of change of control is complete. Every moment of delay is more time for the organisations to drift. It is more time for resistance to build and it is more time without the benefits of the deal. In the next chapter we will look at the timing of the integration period up to the end of the cutover and look at the actions involved.

What makes banking M&A unique

While there are many books written about M&A's and what is required to be successful, few are written from a banking perspective. The regulatory pressures involved are much greater and on the face of it, contradictory. This makes banking M&A unique. Normally the competition regulators are concerned about two aspects of M&A activity. The first concern is whether this deal is anti-competitive. If it is, they will be inclined to prevent the deal from taking place. The second concern is that the deal is conducted correctly in a way that is not detrimental to the shareholders. If the deal were not to happen both firms should be no less able to compete than they were earlier. To make sure this is the case, legislation is in place to effectively keep the two firms apart as much as possible.

What makes banking unique is that the regulators insist that the new firm resulting from the M&A activity is able to trade as a single entity with all its regulatory reporting and risk management from "day one". Because of this, considerable work between the two banks is required and considerable integration and testing is required. This closer working poses a potential risk. Both sides need to be aware of the legal environment existing, and what specific restraints it places on them. For example, in some countries you cannot make any headcount reduction until after the change of control. Future business strategies cannot be discussed or real client data exchanged. All of these constraints need to be understood and communicated early in the M&A process to prevent an unintended regulatory breach.

Managing the integration and change of control period

This section examines the activities and timing involved from the deal being agreed, to the end of the cutover.

Timing and activities

The time it takes a pair of organisations to move from doing a deal to completing the change of control will vary. There are a number of issues that can impact it. Firstly there is regulatory approval to consider, the deal may be considered uncompetitive and not be allowed, but there are also issues of cash and stock management depending on how the deal is financed and the size and complexity o the organisations involved. A large merger or acquisition would typically take five to eight month. For the purpose of illustration, let's assume it is six months.

The timing of major tasks would look something like this:

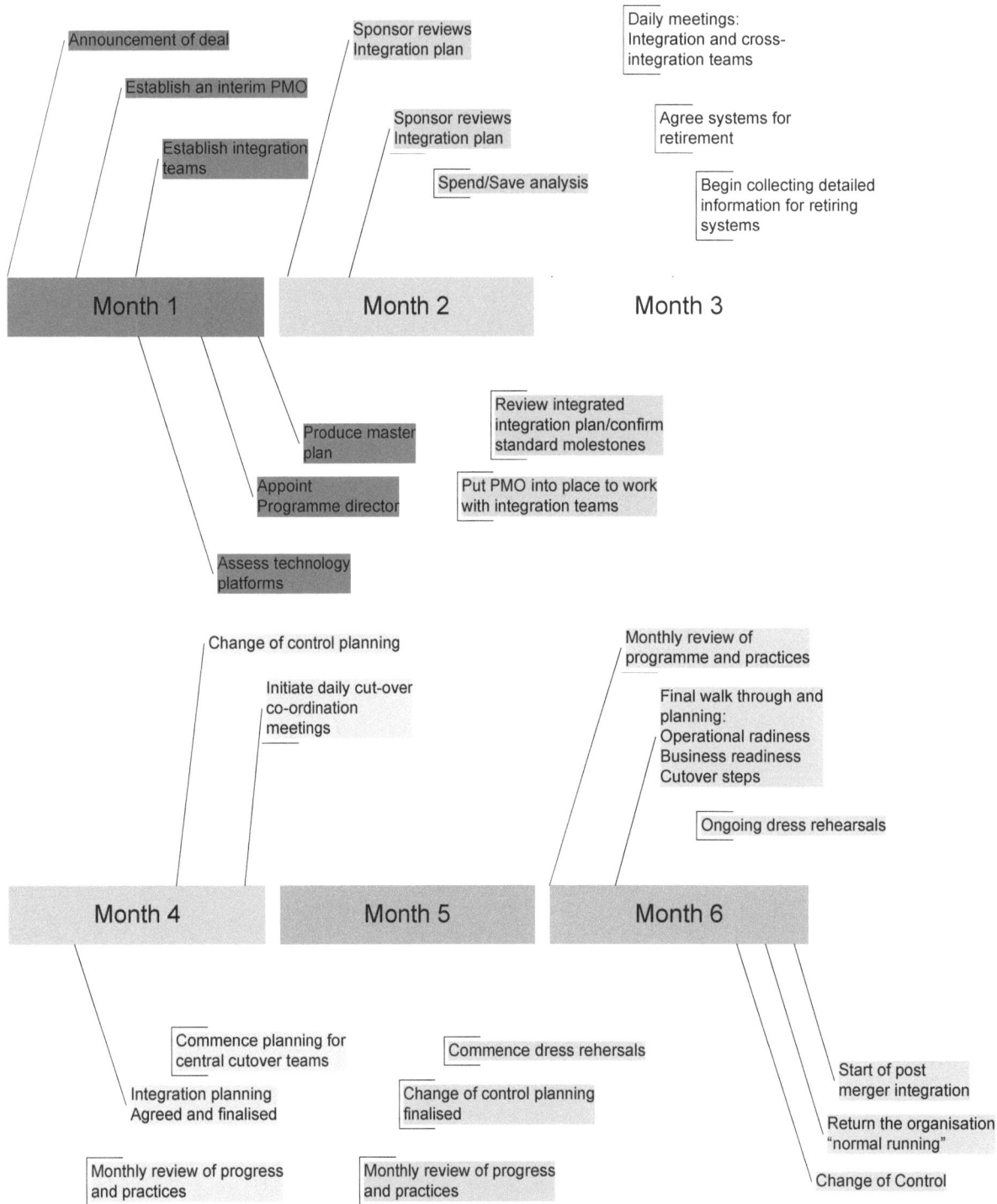

Announcement of deal

Establish an interim PMO

Establish integration teams

Sponsor reviews
Integration plan

Sponsor reviews
Integration plan

Spend/Save analysis

Daily meetings:
Integration and cross-
integration teams

Agree systems for
retirement

Begin collecting detailed
information for retiring
systems

Month 1   **Month 2**   **Month 3**

Produce master
plan

Appoint
Programme director

Assess technology
platforms

Review integrated
integration plan/confirm
standard molestones

Put PMO into place to work
with integration teams

Change of control planning

Initiate daily cut-over
co-ordination
meetings

Monthly review of
programme and practices

Final walk through and
planning:
Operational radiness
Business readiness
Cutover steps

Ongoing dress rehearsals

Month 4   **Month 5**   **Month 6**

Commence planning for
central cutover teams

Integration planning
Agreed and finalised

Monthly review of progress
and practices

Commence dress rehersals

Change of control planning
finalised

Monthly review of progress
and practices

Start of post
merger integration

Return the organisation
"normal running"

Change of Control

Figure 3 - timeline of major tasks

Month 1	
Event	**Description**
Announcement of deal	If a merger is agreed, both firms would typically make a joint announcement. If it is an acquisition. the acquirer might unilaterally make the announcement. At this point the deal may already have the approval of both boards. It would typically be necessary for the shareholders in both firms to approve the deal, but this may depend upon the companies' own rules.
Establish an interim PMO Establish integration teams	Speed is of the essence. An interim project structure is needed across the two organisations. A single PMO needs to be established to initiate the change of control and integration. Their first goals are to: • Establish the programme • Co-ordinate planning • Co-ordinate establishing the integration teams • Put planning and project controls (such as reporting) into place. There is need for a core or central team, and for resources across both firms. There should be a project team or a least a resource at this stage identified for each business unit and geographic area. They will need input from personnel from both organisations. In addition to business units, technology areas and shared functions such as Finance, HR, Legal and Compliance, Audit and so on should also have an initial integration team or contact point.
Assess technology platforms	Even in an acquisition where you are convinced you have superior technology and systems, you owe it to yourself to and your shareholders to identify the best technology. A template needs to be produced and completed for every system in both firms. These need to gather information on issues such as • Technology used • Platforms • Business function Functions • Capacity • Business continuity capability • Location • Business unit supported • Support cost
Appoint programme director	Early on, a senior manager needs to be put in place. The manager should report to the sponsor and the integration steering committee.
Produce master plan	A single master plan for the change of control and integration needs to be established. Each integration team needs to be given a template that will allow them to submit their plans identifying: • Requirement definition (summary at this juncture) • Define their scope • Objectives • Selection platforms they intend to use • How transfers of financial positions will take place • State assumptions • Identify key risks and issues • Present how they will achieve change of control

Month 1	
Event	**Description**
	<ul><li>Schedule<ul><li>Key tasks</li><li>Duration</li><li>Inbound and out bound dependencies</li></ul></li></ul>

Month 2	
Event	**Description**
Sponsor reviews integration plans	The programme sponsor and the steering committee should review the integrated plan. The review should be facilitated by the PMO, but the individual integration teams should present and receive feedback. The programme sponsor may wish an independent third party to review the plan contents also.
Publish first master plan with key dates	Once all this is complete then the PMO is in a position to baseline and publish the plan.
Spend/Save analysis	To get a quick assessment of the financial impact of the M&A transaction all integration teams should complete a spend/save report. This should be structured as appropriate, for the IT organisation it might be by system, for a business line by function and so forth. For each the following is a minimal that mush be identified: • Cost of integration • Cost of systems/process retirement • Cost of organisational changes • Expected cost without the integration • Savings that will be achieved as a result of the integration • New revenue opportunities that can be directly generated as a result of the integration. These typically are marketing synergies to facilitate cross selling for example. This will quickly provide management with a good indication of where savings will be made, or where they will need to achieve greater savings.
Put PMO into place to work with integration teams	At this point the "final" PMO and integration team structure needs to be formalised and implemented.
Review integrated plans/confirm standard milestones	Working with the sponsor and with a target change of control date in mind a defined set of milestones should be agreed and incorporated into all schedules. Once these dates are agreed progress toward them should be widely tracked.

Month 3

Event	Description
Daily meetings: Integration and cross-integration teams	Though regulatory approval may be some way off, the key steps to be taken and how and when they will be achieved are now well established. It is too easy for such a complex organisation to get out of synchronisation with itself. Daily meetings are required to review progress, raise issues and resolve or escalate those issues as necessary. The meetings need to be as short as possible, at a time that is not too inconvenient for everyone (consider that for a global bank daytime where you are, is night time for someone else!) There needs to be a clear structure and format to the meetings in order to keep them focused.
Agree systems for retirement	Based on the systems assessment and their related processes this stage requires the definition of the future state processes and systems. It confirms which systems can be retired. This will lead to longer term cost reductions and therefore attainment of some of the integration goals.
Begin collecting detailed information for retiring systems	For this technical and process details will need to be produced. This will contribute to the ongoing post integration planning. Teams should also identify when they intend to retire the system and reassess the cost and benefits (spend/save).

Month 4	
Event	**Description**
Monthly review of progress and practices	Every month the sponsor and the steering committee review progress being made and adjust any programme practices that require attention.
Integration planning agreed and finalised	The planning needed to prepare the organisations for the change of control needs to be completed to allow the organisations to focus on getting ready for the change of control and the post-change of control integration.
Commence planning for central cutover teams	With a target date for change of control in mind, detailed planning must commence for the cutover weekend itself. A central cutover teem needs to be established. It is responsible for planning and managing the events that will take place over the weekend when the two organisations cut over to the new ownership structure. This requires identification of control points, activities and sign-offs. Additionally, logistical considerations such as staff transport over weekends and unsocial hours, air conditioning, food and cleaning. The central team will also need to establish the central command structure and tools that will be in place over the weekend.
Change of control planning	Once the central teams have established themselves and how they are going to operate, they must extend planning into the integration teams. This is planning as to what will happen during the change of control period. It will need to be in great detail and consider; • What sign-offs are required and when • What data is required and when • Organisational control event • Detailed timings, including time for data to be transmitted, batch runs, creation of accounts and any other activities necessary to enable the change of control.
Initiate daily cut-over co-ordination meetings	Once this detailed planning has commenced, frequent meetings are required to start coordinating the progress and to ensure the necessary data is collected as early as possible.

Month 5

Event	Description
Monthly review of progress and practices	Every month the sponsor and the steering committee review progress being made and adjust any programme practices that require attention.
Change of control planning finalised	Once the detailed planning for the change of control weekend has been completed the organisation can schedule dress rehearsal events.
Commence dress rehearsals	The number of dress rehearsals and there exact scope needs to be agreed by the sponsor. Each event is a "live" enactment of the weekend. As such they are disruptive and expensive. On the other hand not doing a dress rehearsal is very risky. Typically 2-4 dress rehearsals are required. With a 2-3 week break in between each.

Month 6	
Event	**Description**
Monthly review of progress and practices	Every month the sponsor and the steering committee review progress being made and adjust any programme practices that require attention.
Final walkthrough and planning: Operational readiness Business readiness Cutover steps	Assuming all regulatory approvals have been given the date for the actual change of control can be set. Following this the sponsor needs to be satisfied that operationally and from a business perspective the organisation is ready to cut over and that the organisation knows what it will need to do to enable this at the cutover weekend. Integration teams will need to confirm their criteria for commencing and completing the change of control. Timings for the cutover also need to be confirmed at this point.
Ongoing dress rehearsals	Dress rehearsals continue during the lead up to the final cutover.
Change of control/Cutover weekend	This is the actual process of changing ownership and getting the new integrated organisation ready for the first day of trading as a single entity. There is usually a single go/no-go decision. The cutover commences and once completed the two organisations are integrated and ready to trade.
Return the organisation to "normal running"	Once it can be demonstrated that the change of control and cut over have been completed successfully the organisation can return to its normal running state. The special structures put in place to control the cutover can now be stood down.
Start of post merger integration	With the cutover complete, the actions to achieve the long term benefits of the merger or acquisition can now commence.

In parallel to this activity the organisation should be preparing its longer term post merger plan, which can now be implemented.

Project organisation and control

As described previously there are really three strands of activity initiated by the M&A deal. There is the management of the integration of the two organisations. A special part of that is the change of control week-end, the cutover. Finally there is the post merger integration which will be about attaining the various long term goals of the merger or acquisition. This is not directly in the scope of this book, except where integration planning needs to ensure it is considered.

From the first moment there needs to be a sense of urgency. Time is of the essence. Every day there is not planning and control in place the two firms are drifting, the benefits are postponed, a unified corporate direction is not achieved and rumour and resistance are given time and space to grow.

The first days will be the most difficult. A central team needs to be put in place as soon as possible. They must identify and agree how the integration teams will be organised. Some business areas may be so big as to require two integration teams (for example Cash FX London and Cash FX International or Equities US and Equities International). But generally there will be one per business line. The project management office (PMO) needs to move quickly to identify the key contacts and where there are gaps. There needs also to be integration teams for IT and operations and cross business functions. For each integration team they need to identify an owner in each firm, a leader, and assign a PMO liaison.

Table 1 - Integration Team contacts

Integration Team	Team Owner (Bank A)	Team Owner (Bank B)	Team Leader	PMO Contact point
Business Lines				
Credit/Loans				
Derivatives				
Equities				
Exchange services				
Fixed Income				
FX Cash				
FX Option				
FX Prime brokerage				
Investment banking				
Money markets				
Prime Brokerage				
Private banking				
Cross business function				
Audit				
Client management				
Compliance				
Financial Control				
General Counsel / Legal				
HR				
IT				
Operations				
Risk				
Tax				
Possible attritions				
Control				
Cutover				
Operational readiness				
Static data				

The quick population of the key integration roles (above) will allow a meaningful start to the programme. The exact organisation of the integration teams will depend on the organisations own structure. In addition, some firms will wish to pull together integration teams that are not originated along organisational lines.   These are suggested above:

- Control - works to put in place the necessary plans for centralised control functions, ensure there is compliance with the various regulations at each stage
- Cutover - manages the cutover at the change of control week end. This role will be examined further
- Operational readiness – assists the various integration teams to be operationally ready. Assess the readiness of all areas through assessments and walkthroughs and other measures. Should be assessing and reporting the readiness of the organisations before and after the change of control; and
- Static data – Ensure all data id mapped and transferred between systems, including client and market data.

The regions and country contacts need to be established and linked to the various integration teams. It may not always be necessary for there to be a one-to-one relationship. An agency office in a single location may have one person who will have to act as the point of contact/reference for all integration teams. The degree of spread will depend on the size and distribution of the organisation's geographic spread. It is usually best to start with logical regions and break these down to counties and possibly cities if necessary. The degree to which these regions are subdivided will usually reflect the degree of business a bank conducts in that region. In the following example the banks conduct so much business in London that it is treated as a region in its own right, separate from Europe, also most business in China is conducted in Hong Kong and Shanghai so these are separated from other business activities in China.

- London
- Europe
- North America
- South America
  - Brazil
  - Argentina
  - Others

- Asia
  - China
    - Shanghai
    - Hong Kong
    - Other
  - India
  - Japan
  - Singapore
  - Other
- Australia/New Zealand

These activities lead to a matrix organisation that is centrally coordinated, exists across the two organisations and across all geographies and business lines. It is time to move the organisation forward.

Communications and control infrastructure

It is not really possible to over communicate. Rapid, fluid communications across the organisations is necessary. There may be real technical and infrastructural complexities and constraints that will make this difficult. These need to be overcome by having an externally hosted web site that either organisations can access, or making changes to firewalls that will allow both organisations to access the same data. However it is achieved, a web site or similar tool that can be accessed by all with the appropriate security is needed in order to allow;

- Information to be centrally disseminated
- Documents to be stored and shared; and
- Progress to be tracked.

Naturally, some of this information will be sensitive and commercially valuable. Because of this it is necessary to consider the security aspects that go with having a shared central repository.

Scope of integration teams

The scope of integration teams needs to be clearly defined. The central PMO needs to encourage each integration team to define itself, that definition should look something like this:

Table 2 - Template for integration team definition

Name: Name of the integration team	
Description: Description of the integration teams area of responsibility	
Owner (Bank A): Owner assigned from Bank A for this integration team Owner (Bank B): Owner assigned from Bank B for this integration team	Team leader: Leader of the integration team PMO Representative: Name of PMO person assigned to liaise with integration team.
Objective: The objective/s of the integration team	Approach: The approach the team will be taking for initial integration and to prepare for post-merger integration.
Scope: The product and geographic scope of the integration team	Timeframe: The timeframe and key dates the integration team is working to.

Post-merger considerations

This book does not specifically address the post-merger activities. Generally it is possible to manage it using the more traditional approaches and techniques for organisational change. However, there are two aspects of the post-merger activities that need to be considered in the initial integration period. The first of these is that as much planning and preparation for the post-merger programme should be conducted before the cutover, particularly since people will not want to focus beyond the cutover. It is important the momentum for change is not lost because there are no resources or people to take the change forward. Secondly, the approach to post merger integration could well impact the cutover itself. If Bank A has 100 FX traders and Bank B as 70 FX traders, the decision might be taken that from the first day of trading it is desirable to have all FX traders on a single trading floor and that 150 would be sufficient. This decision has logistical, technical, legal and resource management implications, all of which must be addressed before the post-merger phase will begin.

Planning for the post-merger period

As I said earlier, timing is crucial, not a second should be lost in such a fluid environment. There is plenty that can and should be done prior to the cutover. Imagine you are a large retail bank with thousands of retail branches and you have decided to merge with another large retail bank. You may have a strategy to achieve various cost savings through among other things consolidation of your banking network. If you were agile enough you could;

1. Identify where both banks have branches within, say, a five minute walk of each other, and from this compile a list of locations that are served by "duplicate" branches.
2. For each pair of branches identify the one that best suits your needs.
3. Put in place a plan to close the duplicate branch and if necessary rebrand the non-duplicate branches.
4. If it is allowed prior to the change of control you could organise the staff who will need to retrain for other roles, change branch or take redundancy.
5. You could have a deal to sell the properties to a development or retail firm, subject to the successful completion of the merger; and
6. Have all the logistics, customer communications and other matters ready to commence on the first trading day.

Just think of the advantages for the organisation to be able to move this quickly, the cash from the disposal of excess branches would come in quickly, the cost reductions would be achieved within a few months of the acquisition. The organisation can put the trauma of the change behind itself quickly and move ahead.

To make this happen requires vision, leadership and organisation. Once the processes to legally integrate the two firms has commenced, the sponsor must address these challenges. Doing so quickly and clearly will lead to the rapid progress without undue risk or cost.

Vision

There is an underling rationale behind every acquisition and merger. Management will have set themselves and hopefully widely communicate that rational and the goals that underpin it. They may be growth, cost reduction, market share, geographic spread or defensive for example. Either way, these need to be formed into a vision of the future. It needs to be given to someone to drive them through. Without that clarity, the organisation is heading off on a midnight adventure, without a map, to a place it does not know even exists, and they have their eyes closed! The vision is for the long term

Leadership

Leadership is crucial. It will probably be the single most important factor in the long term success of the merger or acquisition. Whoever leads the post merger integration has to embody the vision and keep it alive. The post merger process can be long and buffeted by the winds of change. Only a strong leader who understands the vision will be able to keep it moving forward and not be distracted by emerging events. The leader is required to have the personality to carry through the change. But a strong "Churchill like" leader is not what is called for here. The leader needs to be able to deal with a wide range of factors ranging from "soft" issues thought to "hard" financial realities.

Organisation

Following the appointment of the leader comes the establishment of the organisation, it has to embody many of the leaders attributes and bring the discipline and controls to allow the leader to stretch into the new organisation and have a positive effect. The organisation will typically be relatively small, working through a programme of change implemented as a series of change projects within various businesses. Its' structure may be business function or organisationally aligned.

It is possible for it to share resources with the initial organisation team. This approach offers obvious benefits, but there is one big risk. If the same people who are focusing at post merger integration are focusing on the initial integration and the change of control it is likely their focus will be on the short term, rather than the long term goals. After all, if there is no change of control, there is no post merger integration. Therefore, if the organisation wants to secure a rapid post merger integration it needs to give it the priority and focused resources it deserves

Impact of approach to the cutover

If an organisation is unclear as to how it will achieve post merger integration, it is likely that it will only achieve the minimal of change and integration benefits at the point of change of control. Typically the risk, compliance and general ledger systems will feed from one bank into another. This is sufficient.

Most banks will look to achieve as much as possible in a "big bang" fashion. For each business line they will see is it desirable to combine the two functions. Naturally the answer will almost usually be yes, this is because if the benefits can be achieved early without significant risk, it will build momentum, secure merger benefits and reduce the chance of cost over-runs. An exception might be a wholesale bank merging with a private bank. They might decide that the customers of the wholesale bank may not wish to change how they work. Therefore the person they deal with for foreign exchange dealing might stay the same and remain in the branch office. That said, they will probably phone the FX deal through to the FX front Office or book it onto the front office system. The private bank will also want to retire its middle and back office. It is often possible to achieve these types of process and system changes for the first day of trading.

When the integration team assess their scope and objectives (see page 30) they should consider could the change be implemented during the cutover period. The decision making process will be different for every M&A and every business line.

Here is an example. Bank A and Bank B are merging. They both have a strong Equities Derivatives business. The number of people working on the trading floor (including support teams) is shown below;

	London	New York	Tokyo
Bank A	200	75	35
Bank B	120	250	40

The banks decide it is best to have everyone trading on a single platform from day one. It means one system can be retired and the risk management process is simplifies. On investigation they discover that Bank B probably has the better platform, but it does not have sufficient capacity to handle the combined trading loads. The decision is taken to use Bank A's system.

It is also decided that it would be better if the traders worked from a single trading floor long term, and so this becomes the goal for the cutover. Investigation shows that non-equities staff in London at Bank A will have to move in order to make space for the trading team from Bank B. In New York there is enough space for everyone to work from the Bank B trading floor. While in Tokyo, neither bank can accommodate the other, meaning they will have to stay where they are in the short term. Immediately these decisions will drive actions that need to be actioned before the cutover;

- Bank A will have to clear 120 desks in London to make space for the people from Bank B
- The Bank B traders need to be trained how to use the Bank A system
- Planning will need to be in place to move 120 people at the cutover in London, and 75 in New York.
- The search for a home for the combined team in Tokyo can begin
- New trading terminals for all the Bank B teams will have to be bought and configured
- Communications between the two Tokyo locations need to be put into place

Planning will also need to be put into place for the cutover, such as;

- Connecting up the New York trading floor to the Bank B system
- Moving trading floor staff in London and New York
- Opening communications between trading floors in Tokyo

These show simple examples of how the post merger objectives can be achieved at the cutover and thus the business can start to benefit. In every business line these possibilities need to be examined. Moving at this pace will often throw up issues, but creative solutions can be found. On one acquisition I worked, on a trading team had to be left "behind" in its former parents building. The solution was to wire the floor into both banks. Install terminals for the new trading system of the acquiring bank. At the change of control the floor was switched from one bank to another. All the old trading terminals removed and the locks (or rather door swipe system) were replaced. Not an elegant solution, but highly effective.

These issues should be considered by every integration team as they plan the period up to and including the cutover. Many potential "show stoppers" will be encountered such as capacity constraints (e.g. number of accounts limits or throughput, regulatory questions, human resources constraints). However, with creative thinking solutions can be found to most of these.

Planning to get to the change of control

Top down planning/bottom up validation and detail

The PMO needs to commence top down planning to address the period up to the expected change of control date. It is important that this is done with a view to ensuring that there is also population of detail and validation from the "bottom up", otherwise there is the risk that this planning is done in isolation. These tasks need to be defined and the dates agreed to which all[2] integration teams are working. While these will vary across organisations, a list of possible milestones would be:

---

[2] There may be reason why some task not applicable to a particular integration team.

- Establish M&A change programme
  - Sponsor and steering committee established
  - Central PMO established
  - Integration Teams identified
  - Global project organisation in place
  - Integration teams complete
- Current and first day of trading defined
  - Systems architecture defined
  - Workflow
  - Spend and save analysis complete
  - Systems inventory complete
  - Systems changes defined
  - HR requirements
  - Client relationship requirements identified
  - Custodian/Agent relationship requirements identified
  - Detailed planning for integration completed
  - Staff retention completed
  - Dress Rehearsal plans complete
- Change of control/cutover requirements
  - Position and balance transfer requirements
  - Static data requirements
  - Change of control planning completed
  - Testing plans complete
  - Contingency and PCB planning
  - Detailed plan complete
  - Sign-off
    - Protocol agreed
    - Sign-offs required agreed
- First day of trading
  - Desktop requirements defined

- - Network/infrastructure requirements identified
- Build
  - Systems build complete for cutover
  - Systems build complete for first trading day
  - Static data requirements detailed
- Test
  - Critical systems unit complete
  - Critical systems UAT complete
  - Critical desktop testing for first trading day complete
- Dress Rehearsal
  - Business integration testing complete
  - Dress rehearsal complete
- Operational readiness
  - HR changes complete
  - First trading day client information changes complete
  - First trading day custodial and agent requirements fulfilled
  - First trading day critical moves complete
  - First trading day procedure changes documented
  - First trading day critical systems, interface and desktop changes implemented
- Change of control/cutover
  - Ready to go
  - First trading day static changes implemented
  - First trading day balance transfer complete
  - Cutover complete

A template for the master plan in Microsoft Project 2003 format is available at:
https://www.bankingmandahandbook.com/dload/MasterPlanTemplate.mpp

For each milestone a description and list of deliverables needs to be defined. Samples of these are
presented below;

Establish M&A change programme		
Milestone	**Description**	**Deliverable**
Sponsor and steering committee established	A sponsor for the overall integration is appointed. A steering committee drawn from the two organisations is appointed.	Name of sponsor and steering committee
Central PMO established	Central team established. Staffing, roles and responsibilities are agreed. Project standards defined, may include: • Communications plan • Stakeholder analysis • Issues management process • Risk management process • Estimation guidelines • Reporting standards • Budgeting process	Project team list Procedures and templates created
Integration Teams identified	The names of the integration team are agreed – owners and leaders	Name of integration team contact points
Global project organisation in place	The complete organisation structure across integrations and geographies is in place and operational.	Contact list for all participants
Integration teams complete	Integration leaders confirm teams are in place	Names provided to central PMO

Current and first day of trading defined

Milestone	Description	Deliverable
Systems architecture defined	System flow diagrams, by product, location and entity are mapped. This is for the current systems and the first trading day.	System architecture document.
Workflow	Workflows for the current business and the combined business model on the first day of trading are identified and defined. These should, in total, cover the full lifecycle of all products from trade capture through P&L[3], risk management to the general ledger and MIS[4].	Workflows and signoff by stakeholders.
Spend and save analysis complete	Spend and save information is collected for all areas, showing spend and savings plus headcount information. The PMO or Finance teams can provide initial estimates of cost and benefits.	Spend and save analysis is sent to the PMO to be stored in a non-public part of the Central Repository.
Systems inventory complete	Complete inventories for hardware and software systems, plus their interfaces. Should indicate: • Retirement schedule • Resources • New interfaces or resources required • Assumptions • Technical & fictional requirements	Following a peer review there will be completed inventories and interfaces.
Systems changes defined	Requirements for systems changes, identifying, • Reason for the change • Functional requirement • Technical requirement • Effort/duration • User sign-off of requirement	Stored in Central Repository. PMO ensures the change is authorised and included in the integration team's plan.

---

[3] Profit & Loss
[4] Management Information Systems

Current and first day of trading defined

Milestone	Description	Deliverable
HR requirements	All HR requirements for the first day of trading are completed. • Identify headcount changes • Validation of current and future headcounts • Retention in place and necessary resources identified. • Any impacts of business decisions (e.g. a change to the workflow) and their impact on the headcount requirement or any special HR management required. • Current and future organisational charts	Stored in a confidential part of the Central Repository. HR requirements • Funding • Staff movements • Retention identified and agreed. • Reductions identified and agreed.
Client relationship requirements identified	Where there are common clients ensure they are managed in an integrated fashion. Review and novate contracts and master service agreements. Identify and document differences in client management practices or procedures.	Requirements documented and stored in Central Repository with a plan to manage client changes.
Custodian/Agent relationship requirements identified	Identify changes required to using clearing agents and custodians. Document requirements.	Custodial plans should be provided as appropriate by the integration teams.
Detailed planning for integration completed	Integration plans produced and signed off.	Should include a project schedule and other pertinent items. A sample template can be down loaded at: https://www.bankingmandahandbook.com/dload/IntegrationTemplate.doc
Staff retention completed	Identification of staff to receive retention benefits are finalised and authorised.	HR has a staff retention plan to implement.

Current and first day of trading defined

Milestone	Description	Deliverable
Dress Rehearsal plans complete	Detailed plans for the dress rehearsals are completed	<ul><li>Staff contact lists</li><li>Working rotas</li><li>Logistics</li><li>Communications agreed</li><li>Escalation procedures</li><li>Business continuity plans finalised</li><li>Security procedures</li><li>Transport</li><li>Working environment considerations<ul><li>Air conditioning</li><li>Food and drink</li><li>Office cleaning</li><li>Rest areas</li></ul></li><li>Schedule of tasks</li></ul>

Change of control/cutover requirements

Milestone	Description	Deliverable
Position and balance transfer requirements	The positions and balances that will require transfer of the first day of trading of the new organisation.	Statement of positions signed by respective heads of businesses
Static data requirements	Conduct analysis to locate and identify all static data in both organisations. Identify possible gaps/overlaps and differences. Define necessary procedures to address the differences, or translate data as required.	Mapping defined. Details defined to address differences and gaps.
Change of control planning completed	The planning for the change of control is completed. PMO to define requisite quality for cutover plans.	Each integration team has a change of control plan in place. Individual change of control schedules are brought into a single "cutover" schedule with dependencies and so forth defined.
Testing plans complete	Scope of testing (systems, processes and business areas) is defined. Test environments defined. Test schedule agreed, in particular for integrated testing.	Test packs containing plan, scripts and expected results, are produced. Appropriate sign-off for test packs exists.
Contingency and BCP planning	Contingency plans need to be produced for the cutover period and the first day of trading. These plans need to be clear and understood by those who may have to execute them.	Workarounds and planned escalations defined. Where BCP plans already exist these should be referenced. Plans should be developed in conjunction with the BCP organisation, if one exists.
Detailed plan complete	Detailed planning for the cutover is completed. Dress rehearsals will result in updates, but now the organisation can start to get familiar with the way the real cutover will progress, and its timings.	Detailed, integrated plans and schedules.
Sign-off - Protocol agreed	The points where sign-offs will take place need to be	List of sign off points with the corresponding sign-off sheets.

Change of control/cutover requirements

Milestone	Description	Deliverable
- Sign-offs required agreed	defined. In addition they need to define what criteria will be required for each, and add those to the detailed schedule. Finally the protocols for handling the sign-off sheets need to be defined (e.g. will they be brought to a central coordination centre or faxed?).	Protocols defined on how to handle the sign-off sheets.

First day of trading

Milestone	Description	Deliverable
Desktop requirements defined	Desktop requirements where people will need new desktop systems or access to new applications on their desktops have been defined and a plan exists to facilitate that. As it may involve new hardware, orders may well need to be placed in advance of the first day of trading.	Plan to install new desktops or applications as required or a plan to update desktops as required. Must identify people and locations requiring desktop changes in addition to the resources providing the service.
Network/infrastructure requirements identified	Any changes to the network infrastructure need to be identified and authorised. This could include adding network ports, opening firewalls and so forth.	As above. A procedure should be agreed in advance where emergency work is needed, such as making an unscheduled change to network or opening a firewall.

Build		
Milestone	**Description**	**Deliverable**
Systems build complete for cutover	For the major systems new functionality or interfaces added to facilitate cutover. This might include conversion tools.	Build applications ready for testing
Systems build complete for first trading day	For the major systems, new functionality or interfaces added to facilitate the first day of trading.	Build applications ready for testing
Static data requirements detailed	Data reviewed. Data for conversion identified. Determine how to handle account duplication, if this is not desirable	Static data changes identified and documented. Changes to be made to static data changes should be defined.

Test		
Milestone	**Description**	**Deliverable**
Critical systems unit complete	All critical systems are unit tested.	Detected defects "bugs" addressed. Tests signed off.
Critical systems UAT (User Acceptance Test) complete	All critical systems are UAT tested.	Detected defects "bugs" addressed. Tests signed off.
Critical desktop testing for first trading day complete	All applications to be used on the desktop are tested.	Application and connectivity issues resolved. Tests signed off.

Dress Rehearsal

Milestone	Description	Deliverable
Business integration testing complete	End to end testing of processes and systems for change of control.	All business aligned integration teams sign-off acceptance of the conversion criteria. Any issues raised are addressed in an action plan.
Dress rehearsal complete	Completion of end to end testing of processes and systems for change of control.	All business aligned integration teams sign-off acceptance of the dress rehearsal and its criteria. Any issues raised are addressed in an action plan.

Operational readiness

Milestone	Description	Deliverable
HR changes complete	All staff notifications have been communicated	Retention packages issued. Severance packages administered in accordance with local legislation. Offers or employment distributed.
First trading day client information changes complete	Any changes to client contracts, notifications required have been completed.	Client management team confirm this has been done.
First trading day custodial and agent requirements fulfilled	Any changes to agent or custodian contracts have been identified and agreed.	Any new procedures or protocols are documented, distributed and understood.
First trading day critical moves complete	Any critical moves of staff for the first trading day, such as desks, PCs, telephones have been completed.	Necessary staff have been moved, or their move is in the cutover plan.
First trading day procedure changes documented	Changes to workflows and procedures are understood.	Changes identified. New procedures defined. Work arounds are defined where required. Staff have been trained in the new procedures.
First trading day critical systems, interface and desktop changes implemented	Critical systems are tested and available for the first trading day.	System changes complete. Systems available. Desktop updates.

Change of control/cutover		
Milestone	**Description**	**Deliverable**
Ready to go	Areas are ready to go.	There are defined criteria for being ready for the change of control. Criteria are signed off.
First trading day static changes implemented	All static data changes are made and new data is available.	Integration teams confirm static data is OK
First trading day balance transfer complete	All risk positions and all balances are transferred to the correct systems, usually a single platform for the given product.	All business teams that are transferring positions confirm they have transferred all positions, and requisite checking and reconciliation is complete.
Cutover complete	All integration teams confirm they have completed their cutover activities.	All cutover activities are completed.

Tracking and reporting

During the pre-change of control phase, reporting needs to focus primarily on progress and issues. This section describes a typical reporting regime and some considerations to keep in mind when devising your own reporting regime.

Information needs

It is surprising how often reporting is designed and produced without any consideration as to the recipients needs. It is crucial to consider who needs what, when they need it and how detailed they wish it to be. In addition, consideration also needs to be given to the frequency and difficulty of gathering the information for reporting. If it is too much, it will slow down the project, too little and it is of little use.

Because of the mission critical nature and the high risk of failure the PMO needs to be constantly tracking tasks and their progress. Therefore, task duration needs to be limited. A good rule of thumb is that a task should be no longer than 1 week in duration. If a task is longer than this it should become a sort of summary or master task and have sub tasks less than or equal to 1 week in duration. This forces planning down to a certain level of detail that encourages transparency. If this is the case then tasks will be commencing and completing every day of the project. This progress should be thus reported and processed daily.

Typically, reporting and its frequency might be organised as follows:

Programme progress - Monthly

Critical issue and risks - weekly

Project analysis - weekly

Integration team reports - Weekly

Typically part of a weekly reporting pack

Activities - Daily

Figure 4 - Reporting hierarchy

Variations can be quickly followed up and if there is an issue it can be managed.

Activity Reports

These can easily be collected and updated electronically. Typically the resource performing or the person who manages the delivery of the task will update its progress. Is the task started, has it completed, when did it start, percentage complete and when it is due to complete. If a manual report is produced by the integration teams and submitted centrally, it might look like this:

DAILY TASK UPDATE REPORT

INTEGRATION TEAM NAME					Date of Report: 20 Mar 20XX	
Task No.	Task Description	Baseline Start	Baseline Finish	Actual/Expected Start Date	Actual/Expected Finish Date	Percentage Completed
1	Task 1	1 Jan 20XX	18 Jan 20XX	1 Jan 20XX	18 Jan 20XX	100%
2	Task 2	15 Jan 20XX	3 Mar 20XX	15 Jan 20XX	12 Mar 20XX	100%
3	Task 3	1 Mar 20XX	31 Mar 20XX	7 Mar 20XX	10 Apr 20XX	50%
4	Task 4	1 Apr 20XX	30 Apr 20XX	10 Apr 20XX		0%
5	Task 5	1 May 20XX	31 May 20XX			
6	Task 6	1 Jun 20XX	30 Jun 20XX			
7	Task 7	1 Jul 20XX	31 Jul 20XX			
8	Task 8	1 Aug 20XX	31 Aug 20XX			

Figure 5 - Sample Daily Task Update Report

The integration teams will submit a weekly status report, a typical such report is shown on the following page.

RAG: Red, Amber, Green: Highly visible reporting of overall status.

These criteria must be defined at the start of the programme. Otherwise there is the risk that all reports will be "Green" the whole time.

INTEGRATION TEAM WEEKLY STATUS REPORT

INTEGRATION TEAM NAME	**Date**: DD MM XX
TEAM LEADER: Name	**RAG STATUS :** RED/AMBER/GREEN

TASK STATUS:	SUMMARY
Completed: Tasks completed since the last report ID: Description: Target finish date: Actual finish date	Summary of status for the integration team and its' area of responsibility
Overdue: Tasks which are overdue ID: Description: Target finish date: Expected finish date: RAG Status	**ISSUES/ACTIONS** Major issues and action to address them. Plus indicate if escalation is required. These would typically be reflected in the overall
Next tasks: Tasks to be worked on in the next week ID: Description: Target finish date: Expected finish date: RAG Status	**RISKS** Risks the integration team is particularly concerned about

Figure 6 - Sample Integration Team Weekly Status Report

The weekly project analysis report is an analytical report produced by the BMO. It is largely quantitative and is often used as a counter balance to integration teams own report. It allows senior management to take advantage of the unique perspective the PMO have. A sample is shown on the following page.

WEEKLY PROJECT ANANYSIS REPORT

INTEGRATION TEAM NAME	Date: DD MMM 20XX
TEAM LEADER: Name	RAG STATUS : RED/AMBER/GREEN
ACTIVITY ANALYSIS: RAG Progress: Plan quality: Analysis of the quality of the underlying plans. Typical measures would include: Tasks longer than 1 week duration Tasks with no predecessors Tasks with no successors. Integration team RAG Analysis: A calculated rag status and rag totals for each integration team. Team name: %Red: %Amber: %Green: %Complete: Calculated RAG for overall plan	SUMMARY Summary of status for the integration team and its' area of responsibility
	ISSUES/ACTIONS Major issues and action to address them. Plus indicates that escalation is required. These would typically be reflected in the overall summary above.
	RISKS Risks the integration team is particularly concerned about

Figure 7 - Sample Integration Team Weekly Status Report

This report uses calculated RAG values. These are useful because they are objective. However, they must be carefully defined or they may be the source of great anxiety. One set of rules which I have found useful in defining them is as follows:

If percent complete = 100% then the task is complete (typically Blue)

Else if the expected end date is equal to or earlier than the baseline date then Green

Else if the time the task has slipped (expected finish date minus baseline finish date) is less than or equal to the amount it can still slip by (sometimes called the float) the task is Amber

Else the task is RED.

The critical issues and risk is an extract from the PMO issue and risk log. It is populated with issues and risks which integration team cannot manage within their integration teams, or which endanger the change of control or cutover in some way.

WEEKLY CRITICAL RISK AND ISSUE REPORT

	Date: DD MMM 20XX
CRITICAL ISSUES: A list of all the critical issues. Typical data would include: • Issue number • Issue Description • Who identified it • When it was identified • Actions to resolve • Target resolution date	**CRITICAL RISKS:** A list of all the critical risks. Typically would include: • Risk number • Risk description • Impact • Probability • Action to mitigate • Target date to resolve

Figure 8 – Weekly Critical Risk and Issue Report

The final report is the monthly summary. This needs to be tailored to the needs of the senior executive. Typically it will be similar to the weekly reports, and would be reviewed at monthly steering committee meetings. It will also include financial information on current spend, future spend and likely savings.

The cutover

So far, our focus has been on preparation for integration. This section addresses how the change of control and cutover themselves are managed. This is a very special period. In a short period usually not starting until the close of business in New York and ending with the start of business in Tokyo the banks must:

- Rebrand stationary and possibly buildings and other branded items
- Move all its financial positions to single platforms
- Ensure it can complete its' regulatory reports
- Ensure risk and compliance are able to function for the whole firm; and
- Integrate key systems across the two enterprises. Usually this means ensuring all trading systems feed into a single general ledger. Though sometimes it may be more complex than that.

Planning

Before planning can begin, and this applies to the dress rehearsals also, it is important to consider how the plan and its' tasks are going to be used. There are a number of attributes of the cutover that should be considered.

- Time zone – Almost every cutover involves locations in more than one time zone. Since most project planning tools do not take this into consideration it will be necessary to agree on one time zone for planning, and once decided, disseminate the information widely. Typically most organisations are happy to agree on Greenwich Mean Time (GMT) or the local time of the majority of the organisation, if the majority of participants live in one time zone.
- Minute/Hour planning – Usually we are used to planning to the nearest day. Due to the short execution period planning is typically to the hour, and sometimes to the minute. Therefore, you need to make sure your planning tools can handle this (most can) and you know how to use that facility (most do not).
- Rate of progress – With so many tasks happening over such a short space of time, it becomes clear that tracking of progress and management of issues needs to be done in real time. This means that emailing update sheets is not a practical solution.
- Real time issue management and rapid escalation will be required to address problems so as not to delay the progress of the weekend's events.
- Reporting of progress to senior management and to the broader community needs
- Synchronisation – Real-time enterprise wide synchronisation becomes an issue. Can the end of day batch in London run? Only if we have received and verified the necessary feeds. There may also be many one off manual activities. Sooner or later synchronisation will become an issue. People will need to understand they cannot commence some activities without being told from a central co-ordination centre that the predecessor activities have been completed.
- Finally, there needs to be clear accountability for certain key tasks, such as agreeing the value of assets. Therefore the need to formalised sign-off of key tasks is crucial.

The combination of these various constraints requires a different approach to planning and organising the cutover.

Before the plan can be constructed, thought will need to be given as to how its' usage will impact on the way it is constructed. The PMO will need to be able to take individual plans from business, technology and operation areas typically following the integration team structure. In addition each task will need to have "meta data" to facilitate the overall plan, which could easily contain 5,000 to 10,000 activities, to be "sliced and diced" in various ways in order to meet the reporting and tracking needs of the cutover. Most major project planning tools have the ability to associate such data as a group or flag to the tasks in the file. Step 1 is to define the type of reporting likely to be required and then produce a template to support it. Typically it will be necessary to report, filter, track and print the cutover in many ways. Many of these will be unique to the way the organisations are organisationally and operationally organised, and where they see the risks. Some generic requirements may be:

- View tasks by business area – tagging by business or integration team
- View tasks by geography – tagging the location the task will be performed in. This could be region, country, city, building or datacentre.
- View tasks by business process – of which the task is in support of. An activity performed by operations may be in support of reconciliation activities of Finance and Compliance.
- View by reporting level – How significant the task is. The executives may want to see "Level 1" tasks. The coordination centre "level 2 tasks" and so forth.
- By owner – The owner of the task
- External tasks – If the task is preformed externally to the two organisations.

A template should be produced to incorporate the tagging necessary and standardise the way planning will take place. This should then be distributed and should be accompanied by training or documentation to allow the plans to be constructed correctly. This allows the cutover (or dress rehearsal) plan to be constructed.

The plan needs to be widely disseminated and understood. Sadly, the only real way to do this is to organise "walk through" meetings of the plans. This process allows everyone to understand not just what he or she must do, but how it fits in with everything else.

In addition to communicating the plan there is a large amount of logistics planning and communications. The PMO must gather and distribute accordingly the following data. For key personnel and areas it is best to print and bind this data. While it is difficult to over communicate, consideration should be given to the financial and environmental impacts of giving everyone a "cutover pack". Also certain details that will be required by central coordination team, such as home and mobile phone numbers should also not be distributed too widely. The "integration pack, should contain information, such as:

- Contact details
    - to receive updates, if there is an update "hotline"
    - for any control centres - including telephone and fax.

- o   Other contact details as appropriate
- Contact details for help lines, such as infrastructure, IT support and so on.
- List of locations involved and any time zone considerations.
- The global control structure. This allows them to understand how information is to flow.
- Defined escalation process
- Staffing rosters
- Security information
- Catering information
- Transport
  - o   Travel policy in place
  - o   Taxi arrangements
  - o   Parking
- Air conditioning
- Services
- Rest areas
- Maps and addresses
- Health and safety information

Organisational approach

Cross enterprise control that is flexible enough to be responsive across under these circumstances needs to be clearly defined. At its' heart are the global coordination centre and the executive control centre.

The executive control centre is where the senior executive make decisions and receive their reports and updates. The coordination centre is where the cutover is coordinated and the organisation is kept synchronised. The centre accepts updates, manages the issues that do not require executive input and sends out updates and status reports. It is the focal point for all sign-offs.

The two control areas need to be relatively close, but at the same time executives need to be kept clear of the co-ordination centre for fear they interrupt its operation. Supporting the central coordination team are regional centres, say North America, Europe/Africa and Asia/Oceania. These will be fed into regional and business integration teams.

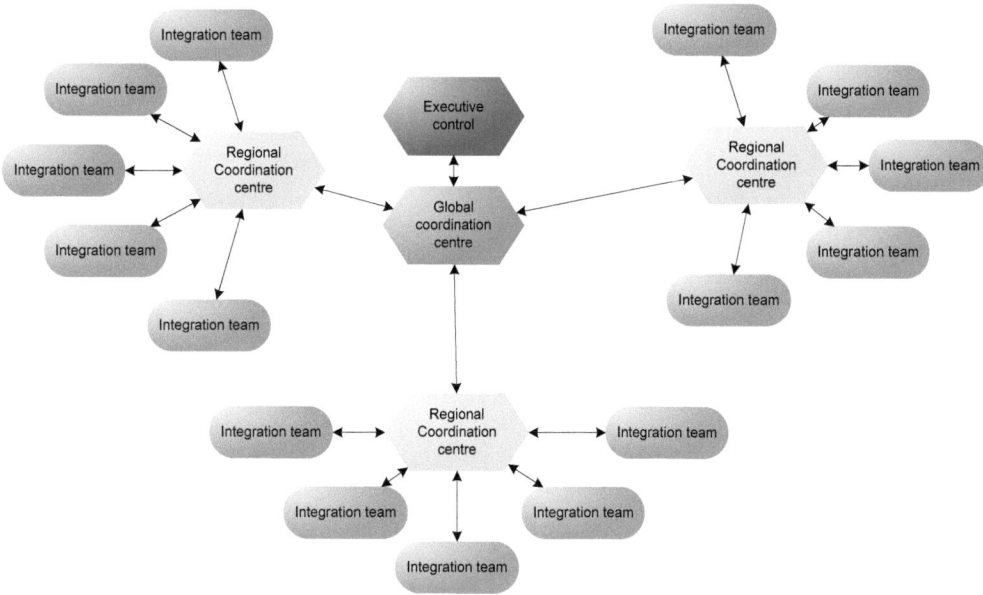

Figure 9 - Sample control centre typography

Depending on the size of the organisation this could be simplified to have integration teams report directly into the central co-ordination centre.

Another approach is to have related integration teams feeding into appropriate coordination centres. These in turn feed into the central coordination centre and this into the executive coordination centre. These two typographies are illustrated in Figure 9 - Sample control centre typography and Figure 10 - Second sample control centre typography.

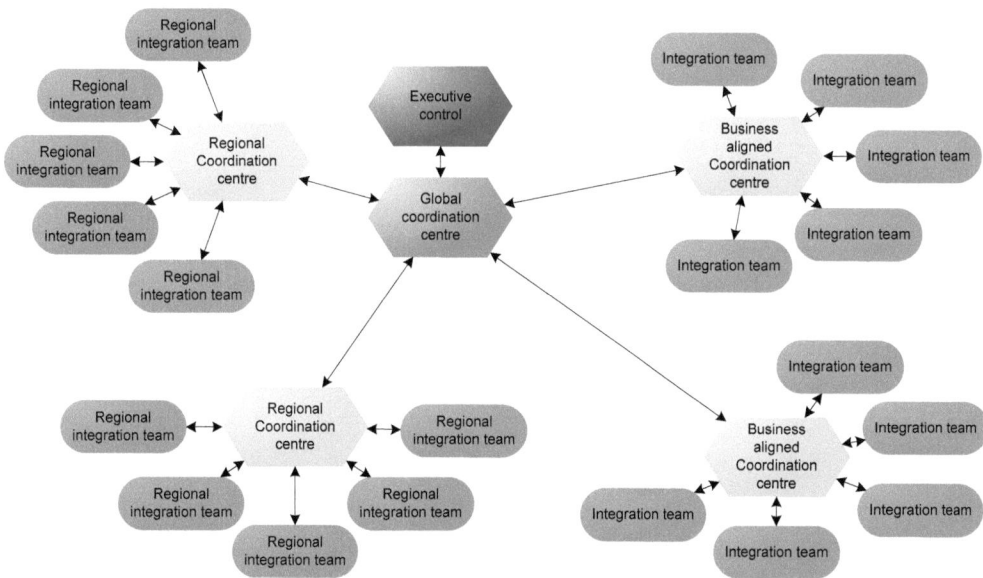

Figure 10 - Second sample control centre typography

Roles and responsibilities

Executive control centre
- Resolves critical issues, as needed
- Monitors significant decisions made by the Steering Committee or in the Command Centre
- Consults with and apprises the full steering committee and business units of significant issues during the cutover weekend
- Makes decisions on significant issues

Coordination centre
- Monitor progress against cut-over plan
- Accumulate and disseminate information related to the cut-over
- Raise issues and questions to the Cut-over Steering Committee Leadership
- Monitors sign-off from the integration teams, other controlling teams and business units

Integration teams/Regional teams
- Execute detailed cut-over plans
- Report progress against key deliverables to the coordination centre

Infrastructure

To manage the cutover effectively, and to ensure it is implemented efficiently an infrastructure needs to be provided to allow progress tracking and issue management to take place efficiently in real time.

Typically you want some form of central website that everyone can access and update their plan task from. Otherwise you will need to track these by telephone or paper update, which is expensive and prone to error. The central site should include things such as:

- Updated plans (with the ability to continually appraise and change)
- Milestone Reports
- Status Reports
- Issues Reports
- Contact Details
- Control Document
- Cutover tasks packs
- Business continuity plans

To make this happen effectively and efficiently a toolset needs to be put into place which can track all the events and record their timings (particularly important if something goes wrong in address rehearsal, as it makes investigation so much easier). It is also important that everyone sees the correct level of detail, so someone working on a task needs to see their own tasks along with those of predecessors and successors. The central coordination team need to be able to see all tasks, but generally should focus on the crucial ones, such as sign-offs and cross integration team co-ordination teams, thus leaving the co-ordination teams to manage their own tasks. It is best this is all achieved in a single toolset. The structure and flow of information in such a tool set is shown in the following illustration.

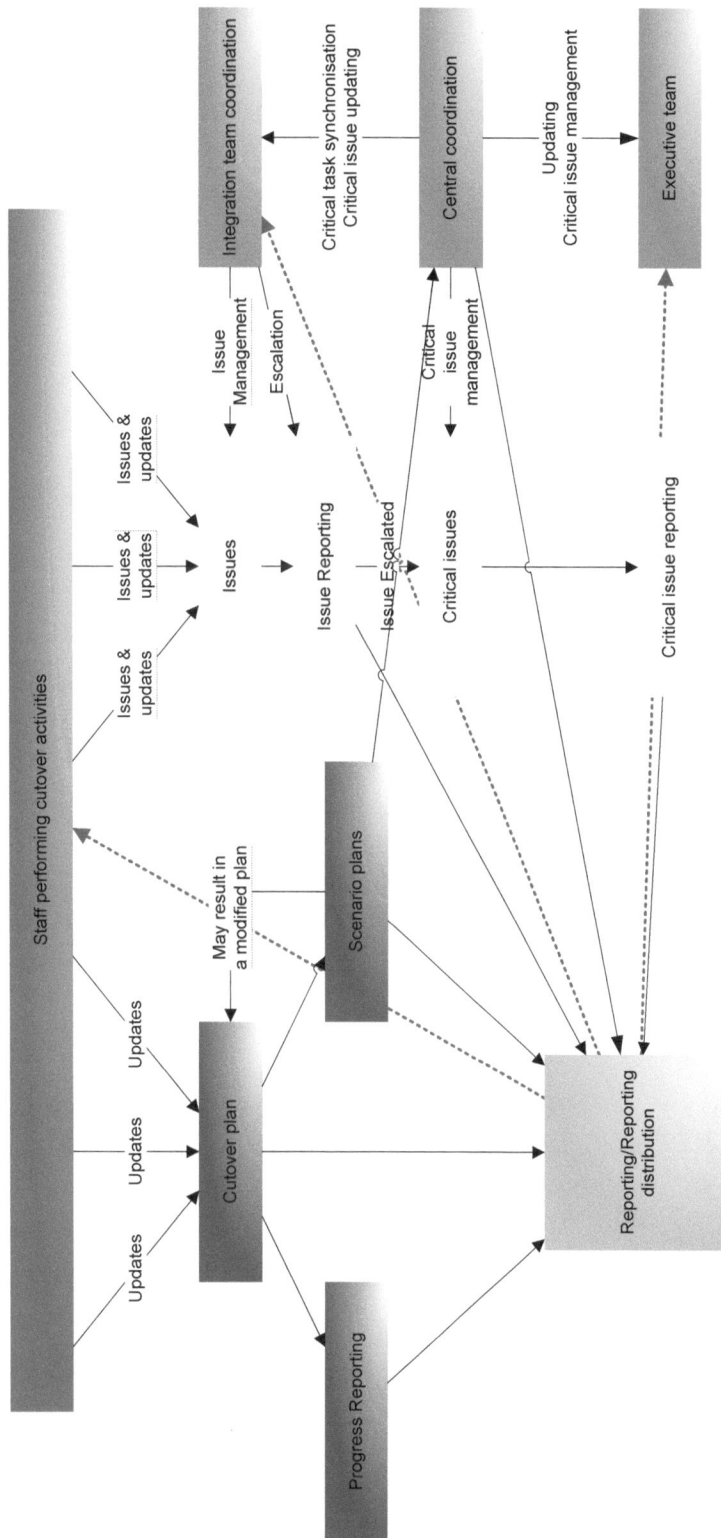

Figure 11 - Cutover control infrastructure

Staff performing cutover activities

Over the cutover weekend 100's and frequently 1000's of staff across the two enterprises will perform the necessary tasks to facilitate integration. They need to use the cutover infrastructure to record their progress. At a minimum they should update the activity when they;

- Commence a task – Let central and integration teams know the task is underway
- Complete a task - Let central and integration teams know the task is complete
- Become aware that the task may take more/less time than expected – Allow rescheduling to reflect the most likely outcome for a task.

Additionally, the central tool, with or without input from the central control team (depending on the priority of the work) will inform staff when given tasks can commence. This can be facilitated in various ways, and a robust coordination centre will be able to accept updates in more than one way. Typical methods would include;

1. Online entry – most preferable due to number of tasks involved
2. Telephone - Telephoning the integration coordination team or central co-ordination team who would then update the cutover plan; or
3. Fax – Sending written updates to the integration coordination team or central co-ordination team who would then update the cutover plan.

Staff can also raise and update issues. The management of these issues is with the area's integration coordination team. This is described a little later on.

Cutover plan

The live updating of tasks updates the cutover plan. This enables the plan to reflect the current situation. This allows real-time, or near to real time reporting on progress. Because of this the plan is dynamic. It requires a controlled process to reassign tasks, change dependencies, even re-plan activities. Most modern planning tools allow this.

Scenario planning

Frequently the coordination centre will want to create a copy of the plan and perform some analysis such as, 'what happens if the sequence of task is changed, or timings are extended'. This type of "what if" analysis will frequently be required and so the control centre must be able to perform it. It helps to answer questions such as; 'What activities will be impacted if the transfer of accounts will take four hours later than expected'?, or drive practical decisions such as, 'what time should financial control staff be called in to perform reconciliations, if the overnight batch finishes 3 hours early'.

Progress reporting

The demands for progress reporting are very varied. This is one of the biggest challenges for any reporting tool sets. A typical set of reporting requirements and who might they be made available to would be:

Reporting	Audience				
	Executive team	Central Coordination team	Integration Coordination team	Integration team members	General staff
Summary progress	Yes	Yes			Yes
Summary tasks about to start	Yes				Yes
Summary tasks about to complete	Yes				Yes
Detailed tasks about to start		Yes -all	Yes – integration team	Yes – for that member	
Detailed tasks about to complete		Yes -all	Yes – integration team	Yes – for that member	
Tasks overdue to start		Yes -all	Yes – integration team	Yes – for that member	
Tasks overdue to complete		Yes -all	Yes – integration team	Yes – for that member	
Critical Path	Summary	Detailed	Detailed – integration team area		

This reporting feeds into the central mechanism for report storage and distribution.

Issue management

Issue management is about identifying, classifying and managing issues, which occur during the project's life cycle. Generally the issue management deals with events that are having a negative impact on the project; however, it can also be used to manage the capture of opportunities that present themselves.

> **Definition:** An issue is an event that has occurred or is occurring. The issue can negatively impact the project's ability to successfully attain its goals, or may be an opportunity that, if not seized, will result in the project not being able to improve its performance.

The key challenges for a cutover event are that issues are managed quickly; hence the need for an electronic automated solution and ensure issues are clearly and quickly escalated if needed. The integration coordination team should normally manage issues. However, if an issue requires cross integration team management, requires an executive decision or threatens the timing of the cutover event it should be escalated to the central coordination team, who may or may not escalate it to the executive team as required.

Purpose of the issue management process

Issues are unplanned events that have already occurred, or are in the process of occurring. If not addressed, these will result in the project being negatively impacted, or in the project missing an opportunity to enhance its delivery. The management of issues is important because issues which are left unmanaged will, in time, reduce a project to potential failure. A successful issue management process will achieve a number of goals:

- Issues are identified
- The impact and effort to address issues is quantified
- Issues are prioritised appropriately
- Ensures management attention is focused on issues that warrant management attention
- Management attention is directed in a focused and prioritised manner
- Issues the project is facing are communicated clearly
- There is a consensus as to the issues and priority of issues to be managed.

The issue management process

The issue being managed by the issue management process will pass through a number of stages as defined by the central cutover team. Typically this might be in the order of seven stages in its lifecycle. In addition to those the issue may be placed on hold (to be addressed post cutover or deemed not an issue that can be mitigated.

Pre formal management

In this stage a member of the project, or stakeholder, identifies what they believe to be an issue. In order to ensure this is an actual issue, and that it is unique, i.e. not raised before, the issue needs to be assessed by an authorised assessor. Projects will typically have a number of individuals who are authorised to assess and formally raise issues. If the authorised assessor believes the issue to be of sufficient significance and to be unique they will formally create an issue. If not they explain the reason for their decision to the person who identified the issue (issue raiser) in the first instance.

New issue

This is the first formal stage. The authorised assessor informs the project's issue manager they are going to raise an issue. The issue manager adds this to the project log and assigns the issue an issue tracking number (the issue number). If necessary the issue manager will provide the authorised assessor with a blank issue form also. The authorised assessor and the issue raiser will complete the issue form (see Appendix 1) and submit it to the issue manager. The issue manager will file the issue form. The issue now becomes "Open".

Open issue

The first task for the issue manager is to find a resource who can evaluate the issue, assess its impact and outline a recommendation to address it. The recommendation will typically be:

- A series of steps to address the issue and eliminate or at lease reduce its' impact
- An assessment that this is not actually an issue
- A recommendation that the issue should not be addressed either on the grounds of cost or project risk.

Once a resource has been found, and the issue evaluator is prepared to accept the issue, the issue is assigned to them. Once they have completed their evaluation, the issue form is updated accordingly and the recommendation or recommendations are submitted for approval by the issue management board.

The issue manager reviews and presents the issue to the issue management board. The issue management board reviews the issue and makes one of the following approval decisions:

- Not approved – The issue is not approved; in effect the board do not consider it to be an issue. The issue is "not approved". This decision is communicated to the issue raiser.
- More work required – The management board require more information or preparation to be conducted before they can make a decision on the issue. The issue is returned to the issue evaluator for more work.
- Close issue – The board decide not to take any specific action on this issue.
- Approve to progress – The board approve an action or set of actions to resolve the issue. The approved action may be substantial and the board may feel that to take the action will cause the project to move out of governance. In this situation the planned action will be to raise a change request, see the change request process.

In progress

This stage is where the issue is addressed. Now that the issue has been approved for resolution the issue manager updates the issue log accordingly. The resource to perform the work is identified and the work scheduled. There may be more than one stakeholder involved. The issue manager may, depending on the size of work have to treat this as any planning effort. On the other hand the issue manager may be able to simply "have the work done" if it is sufficiently minor and provided doing so has no impact on the project schedule. If there is an impact on the schedule, its' impact will have been identified on the evaluation.

The work, which now has an identified schedule and resource or resources, is undertaken. Once done the person resolving the issue informs the issue manager that the work is complete. The issue manager needs to be satisfied the solution resolves the issue and should test it to some degree, if possible, passing it back to the person who raised the issue if the solution is insufficient or misunderstood.

If satisfied, the issue is deemed to be completed.

Completed

In this state, the Issue raiser reviews the issue and its' solution, to determine if it is a satisfactory solution. If not, the issue is returned.

Note: Human nature being what it is, people can sometimes be overly demanding. The issue raiser may demand a solution that is 100% perfect, which may be beyond the ability of the project to practically deliver in the circumstance. In this situation the issue manager may want the work to pass to the issue management board after the issue raiser has reviewed it, and even though the issue raiser has rejected it. In this circumstance it should be reported to the board the solution to the issue has been rejected and why. The issue management board can then decide on the appropriate course of action.

Closed

Once an issue is closed the issue manager ensures the issue is closed in the issue log, and the issue form is up to date and filed. The issue manager will from time to time wish to review the closed issues to ensure they have not re-occurred.

Other issue conditions

In addition to the various stages of the life-cycle identified here, sometimes the issue may be taken "off process". For example, at any point an issue may be put on hold, for example, to be considered later. Sometimes the issue may be considered to be not an issue and addressed as such, or the issue may be closed once evaluated. Some of these conditions or "states" are shown in the following diagram:

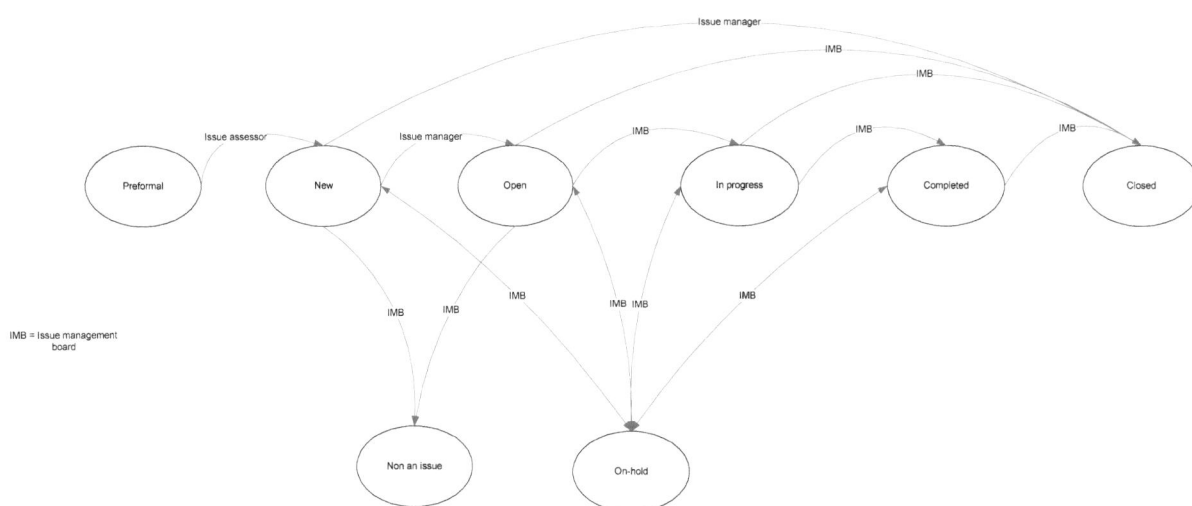

Figure 12 - Issue states

Reporting and distribution

The distribution of reporting needs to be flexible enough to handle changes to the reporting requirements during the cutover. With all reports it is important to identify which reports can be "collected" by their audience and which need to be "sent" to their users, and if so, how. This needs to be identified for every reporting channel.

Reports to be collected could be made available on a web site or a shared folder. Those that need to be sent or "delivered" can be distributed in various forms;

- E-mail the report
- E-mail a link to the report
- Send an SMS message
- Deliver a printout
- Update a progress chart (or progress wall) where a wide audience can see the changes and progress.
- They might be an "on demand" query.

With things moving very quickly it is important that everything is easy to follow and understand. When designing the reporting, focus should be on simplicity of design and ease of use. A "dashboard" approach is frequently preferable to presenting lots of details.

Using modern technology, it is relatively easy to construct this type of infrastructure. It is important not to loose track of what it is actually for. It is to unify communications, and create common understanding of progress and issues. The third function is to allow the organisation to understand current progress and "project" into the future to understand what may be about to happen. Modelling the future state with techniques such as a Monte Carlo simulation and even simpler techniques such as projecting current variations onto future tasks will provide an early warning system. Allowing the organisation time to contemplate responses to a problem in advance of the problem ever actually materialising!
A control or coordination centre is much like a scaled-down version of NASA's mission control. The layout of a small control centre is shown in the figure below:

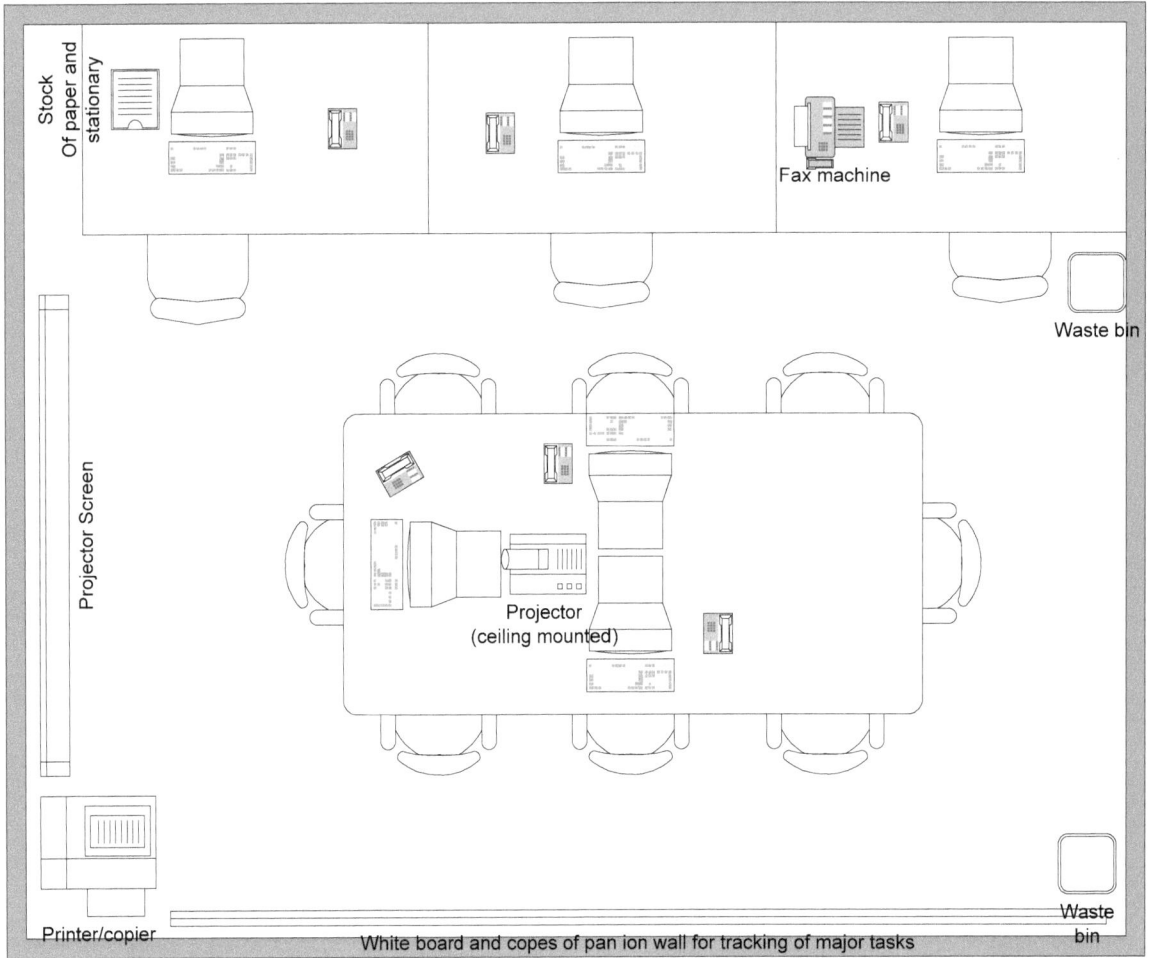

Figure 13 - Layout of a typical control centre

What if it all goes wrong?

Even with the best planning and preparation in the world, unforeseen events can happen. I worked on one M&A deal where during a dress rehearsal a team of men undertaking road works accidently cut all the communications to the London head quarters. But we had a back-up plan and the control centre hardly skipped a beat as we switched to predefined mobile telephones instead.

In the planning all the risks that can reasonably happen, need to be indentified and addressed. Much of this will already be addressed in the BCP planning for the two organisations. The integration teams need to focus on risks that might occur due to the unusual activities of the cutover weekend. Once these have been planned for, one more thing has to be considered. If for whatever reason the cutover were to fail, at any point, how would you back out and how long would it take to get both organisations back to the position they were at, at close of business on the Friday evening.

A back out plan would typically involve activities such as;

- Restoring systems to a defined point at the start of the integration – typically at the end of "end-of-day" processing on the first (Friday) night.
- Connecting/disconnecting networks and PC
- Communicating with the media
- Closing any opening in the firewalls; and
- Moving staff back to their old desks.

The activities are thankfully simple and not difficult to action. The length of time required and the correct sequence needs to be determined in advance. The length of time, because it allows the executive to know when they have run out of time to deal with any issues. If it takes 8 hours to back out and you are 12 hours away from the start of the trading day, you have four hours to try and remedy the situation. If it is 8 hours away, then management can make a risk/reward decision about how long they would be willing not to trade and be out of the market in order to try and remedy the situation.

When you are in this situation you do not want an elaborate discussion about how to back out. It should be known in advance and tested. A good practice is to define in advance what the decision making criteria around backing out would be, and could you back out part of the organisation and let the rest progress with the integration. Obviously, these issues are unique to a given deal, and so there are no hard and fast rules.

Appendix 1 – Issue template

The Project Management Handbook

Issue Form

Project name:

Project Manager:

Issue manager:

Issue Number:

Issue title:

Date raised: Last update: Date closed/resolved:

Status:

Preformal [ ]   New [ ]   Open [ ]   In-Progress [ ]
Completed [ ]   Not an issue [ ]   On-hold [ ]   Closed [ ]
Reporting status: RED/AMBER/GREEN/COMPLETE <- Delete as appropriate

Raised by:

Assigned to:

Detailed description:

Action record

Action number	Date assigned	Assigned to	Description/Status	Date due

© 2006/07 Michael McGrath

Index

www.ingramcontent.com/pod-product-compliance
Lightning Source LLC
Chambersburg PA
CBHW041723210326
41598CB00007B/763

9 780955 985904